OBSIDIAN

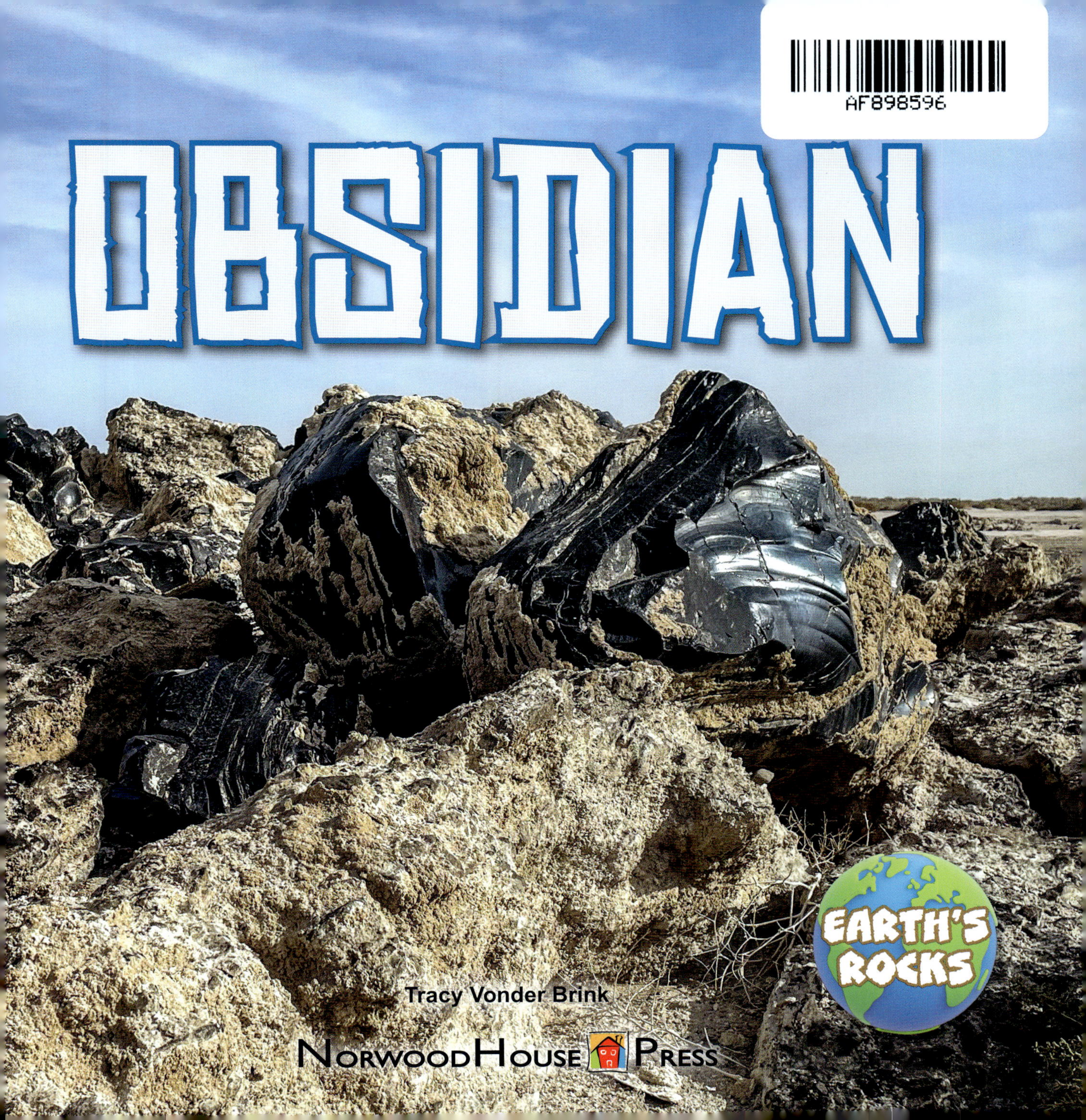

EARTH'S ROCKS

Tracy Vonder Brink

NorwoodHouse Press

Cataloging-in-Publication Data

Names: Vonder Brink, Tracy.
Title: Obsidian / Tracy Vonder Brink.
Description: Buffalo, NY : Norwood House Press, 2027. | Series: Earth's rocks | Includes glossary and index.
Identifiers: ISBN 9781978580145 (pbk.) | ISBN 9781978580152 (library bound) | ISBN 9781978580169 (ebook)
Subjects: LCSH: Igneous rocks--Juvenile literature. | Magmatism--Juvenile literature.
Classification: LCC QE461.V66 2027 | DDC 552.1--dc23

Published in 2027 by
Norwood House Press
2544 Clinton Street
Buffalo, NY 14224

Designer: Rhea Magaro
Editor: Kim Thompson

Photo credits: Cover, p. 1 Gerald Peplow/Shutterstock.com; p. 3 Jirik V/Shutterstock.com; p. 4 Kavic.C/Shutterstock.com; p. 5 ImageBank4u/Shutterstock.com; p. 7 William T Smith/Shutterstock.com; p. 8 BlueRingMedia/Shutterstock.com; p. 9 papa papong/Shutterstock.com; p. 10 SkillUp/Shutterstock.com; p. 11 Martin Korsawe/Shutterstock.com; p. 12 Pung/Shutterstock.com; p. 13 Zigzag Mountain Art/Shutterstock.com; p. 15 Pedro Carrilho/Shutterstock.com; p. 16 Zack Frank/Shutterstock.com; p. 19 wonderisland/Shutterstock.com; p. 20 Bea Kiss/Shutterstock.com; p. 21 Ian Dewar Photography/Shutterstock.com;

Printed in the United States of America

CPSIA compliance information: Batch #CSNHP27: For further information contact Norwood House Press at 1-800-237-9932.

TABLE OF CONTENTS

WHAT IS OBSIDIAN?

Rocks make up many things in the world, from tall mountains to the deep seafloor. All rocks are made of **minerals**. They are put into three main groups based on how they form.

Types of Rock

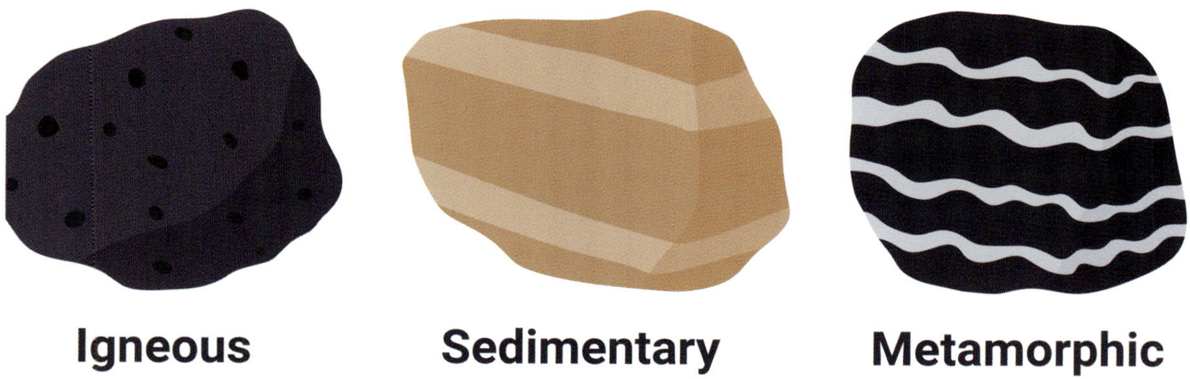

Igneous means "fire." Igneous rocks form from fiery **magma** or lava. Obsidian is an igneous rock.

Obsidian looks like no other rock. That's because it's glass! Obsidian is often a dark, shiny black. It can also be red, brown, or green. Some kinds even look like a rainbow.

HOW DOES OBSIDIAN FORM?

Like all rocks, obsidian forms during Earth's rock cycle.

Part of the rock cycle takes place in Earth's mantle, deep inside the planet. Earth has layers. The crust is on top. The mantle lies below. It's so hot in the mantle that rock melts into magma.

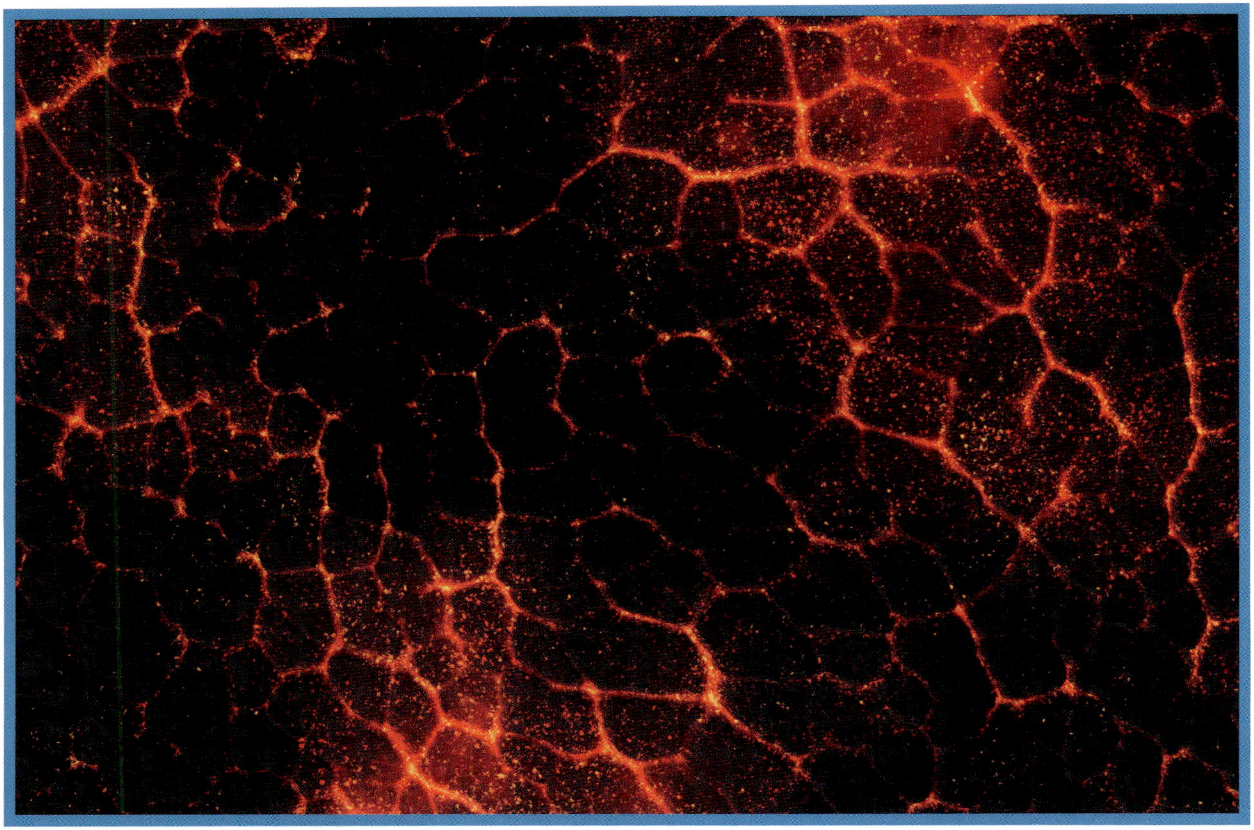

Magma rises because it's less **dense** than the rock above it. Sometimes, it pools underground in areas called magma chambers.

Inside magma chambers, heat and **pressure** can build up. If the ground above is weak or has cracks, the magma may come out through volcanoes.

Lava is magma that reaches Earth's surface. It starts to cool as soon as it touches air or water. Obsidian forms from lava that cools very fast.

Sometimes, when igneous rocks cool more slowly, **crystals** can form. But obsidian has no crystals. The lava cools so fast that there is no time for crystals to form. That's why obsidian is smooth glass.

WHERE IS OBSIDIAN FOUND?

Obsidian comes only from volcanoes that eject magma full of a mineral called **silica**. Obsidian forms near volcanoes all over the world. It has been found in the western United States, Central and South America, Italy, Iceland, and Japan.

Obsidian Cliff is part of Yellowstone National Park in the United States. The cliff stands about 200 feet (60 meters) tall and stretches for nearly half a mile (804 meters). More than 50 feet (15 meters) of obsidian can be seen in its side.

HOW IS OBSIDIAN USED?

Obsidian is sharper than steel. It can be cut and shaped to make very sharp tools.

Ancient people used obsidian for arrowheads and other weapons. Today, it's used to make some **surgical instruments**.

Smooth obsidian has a **distinctive** look. People have used it to make jewelry for thousands of years.

Obsidian is found only in certain places on Earth. This special rock is useful and beautiful.

GLOSSARY

crystals (KRIS-tuhls): substances that form patterns of many flat surfaces as they become solids; quartz and salt are examples of crystals

dense (dens): heavier than many things of a similar size

distinctive (di-STINGK-tiv): different from others; unique

magma (MAG-muh): melted rock below Earth's surface that becomes lava when it flows out of volcanoes

minerals (MIN-ur-uhlz): solids that form naturally in Earth and that do not come from an animal or plant; obsidian contains minerals such as silica and feldspar

pressure (PRESH-ur): the force produced by pressing on something

silica (SIL-i-kuh): a mineral that is made of silicon and oxygen and that is found in sand and quartz

surgical instruments (SUR-juh-kuhl IN-struh-muhnts): tools used by doctors during medical procedures to cut, remove, or repair parts of the body

THINKING QUESTIONS

1. How are rocks put into groups?
2. What does obsidian look like?
3. Why does magma rise?
4. Why does obsidian have no crystals?
5. Describe some of the ways people use obsidian.

INDEX

ABOUT THE AUTHOR

Tracy Vonder Brink is always curious about the world around her. She loves to make facts and true stories fun and has written many books for kids. Tracy lives near Cincinnati, Ohio, and enjoys reading, hiking, and playing with her two rescue dogs.